Smelly SKUNKS

by Catherine Nichols

Consultant: Gabrielle Sachs
Zoo Educator

BEARPORT PUBLISHING

NEW YORK, NEW YORK

Credits

Cover and Title Page, © Steve & Dave Maslowski/Photo Researchers, Inc.; TOC, © Eric Isselée/Shutterstock; 4–5, © John Conrad/Corbis; 6, © Thomas Kitchin & Victoria Hurst/kitchinhurst.com; 7, © Tom Vezo/Nature Picture Library; 8, © Daniel Cox/Oxford Scientific/Photolibrary; 9, © Arthur Morris/Corbis; 10, © Tom Brakefield/Stockbyte/Alamy; 11, © Geoffrey Kuchera/Shutterstock; 12T, © blickwinkel/Brehm/Alamy; 12C, © C. Huetter/Arco Images/Alamy; 12B, © Anthony Mercieca/Photo Researchers, Inc.; 13, © John Downer Productions/Nature Picture Library; 14, © Bruce & Jan Lichtenberger/SuperStock; 15, © Leonard Lee Rue III/Photo Researchers, Inc.; 16, © Jan L. Wassink; 17, © Ronald Wittek/Deutsche Presse-Agentur/newscom.com; 18, © Steve Maslowski/Photo Researchers, Inc.; 19, © Gerald & Buff Corsi/Visuals Unlimited; 20, © R. Wittek/Arco Images/Alamy; 21, © Christof Koepsel/Bongarts/Getty Images; 22, © Simon Wagen/John Downer Productions/Nature Picture Library; 23TL, © Bruce & Jan Lichtenberger/SuperStock; 23TR, © Ronnie Howard/Shutterstock; 23BL, © Galyna Andrushko/Shutterstock; 23BR, © Jan L. Wassink; 24, © Eric Isselée/Shutterstock.

Publisher: Kenn Goin
Senior Editor: Lisa Wiseman
Creative Director: Spencer Brinker
Design: Becky Munich
Photo Researcher: Jennifer Bright

Library of Congress Cataloging-in-Publication Data
Nichols, Catherine.
 Smelly skunks / by Catherine Nichols.
     p. cm. — (Gross-out defenses)
Includes bibliographical references and index.
ISBN-13: 978-1-59716-716-1 (library binding)
ISBN-10: 1-59716-716-9 (library binding)
1. Skunks—Juvenile literature. 2. Animal defenses—Juvenile literature. I. Title.

QL737.C248N53 2009
599.76'8—dc22

                              2008004816

For more information, write to Bearport Publishing Company, Inc., 101 Fifth Avenue, Suite 6R, New York, New York 10003. Printed in the United States of America.

10 9 8 7 6 5 4 3 2

Contents

A Smelly Weapon

It's dinnertime and a group of hungry foxes has spotted a tasty treat—a skunk.

The skunk is too slow to outrun its **enemies**.

So it raises its bushy tail and sprays a stinky oil.

Phew! A horrible smell fills the air.

The oil stings the foxes' eyes.

They can't run away fast enough!

A skunk's oil smells awful! Some people say the odor reminds them of burnt rubber or even rotten eggs!

Under the Tail

All skunks can spray a smelly oil, called musk, when they're in danger.

The musk is stored in two small pouches under the animal's tail.

The pouches hold enough musk for about six sprays.

When the pouches are empty, it takes the skunk a few days to make more musk.

A skunk can spray as far as 15 feet (5 m). The stinky oil can sting enemies' eyes and make them feel sick. The musk is not deadly, but its bad smell can stick around for days!

A Warning

Skunks don't always need to make a stink to keep away enemies.

Often, an animal needs just one look at a skunk's fur to know that it shouldn't get any closer.

The black-and-white color is a warning for animals that have already been sprayed.

They remember the skunk's nasty smell and striped colors.

They know not to mess with a skunk if they don't want to stink!

great horned owl

Great horned owls hunt skunks even after they've been sprayed. These birds have a poor sense of smell and they're not bothered by a skunk's stinky musk.

Scary Skunks

Not all enemies stay away when they see a skunk.

So the skunk first tries to scare off the enemy.

It makes itself look bigger by arching its back and lifting its tail.

It may also stomp its feet and hiss.

If these tricks fail, the skunk sprays its stinky oil.

When a skunk sprays, it bends its body into a U-shape. It does this so that its eyes and tail are always facing the enemy while spraying.

Places to Live

There are four kinds of skunks that live in North America.

Some of these kinds can also be found in South America and Central America.

Skunks live in woods, **grasslands**, deserts, or even in people's backyards.

Though they live in different places, all skunks have one thing in common—their terrible smell!

hog-nosed skunk

striped skunk

hooded skunk

NORTH AMERICA

ATLANTIC OCEAN

PACIFIC OCEAN

CENTRAL AMERICA

SOUTH AMERICA

N W E S

☐ Where skunks live

The spotted skunk stands on its front paws to scare its enemies. It looks like the skunk is doing a handstand.

spotted skunk

Safe at Home

Skunks make their homes in **dens**.

The dens can be in hollow trees or logs, or under buildings.

Skunks also live in underground dens called burrows.

They often use burrows left by other animals.

However, they can also dig their own.

den

Skunks usually live by themselves. Sometimes, however, several will sleep together in a den.

burrow

Baby Skunks

A den is also the place where a mother skunk gives birth each spring.

A skunk can have between two and ten babies, called **kits**.

Newborn kits are helpless.

They are born with their eyes closed, so they can't see.

They depend on their mother for food and to stay safe from enemies.

kits

Kits are able to spray their smelly musk one to six weeks after they're born.

Learning to Hunt

At first, kits drink only their mother's milk.

After about six weeks, their mother shows them how to find their own food.

She teaches them to hunt for insects, earthworms, mice, lizards, and frogs.

They also eat fruits, nuts, leaves, grasses, and bird eggs.

wild turkey eggs

Skunks hunt mostly at night because they can't be in the sun for long periods of time. The sun is too hot and can make them sick. Their sharp sense of smell helps them sniff out food in the dark.

On Their Own

In the fall, the young skunks are ready to go off on their own.

They have learned how to take care of themselves.

They can find places to live and they know how to hunt.

They also know how to avoid being eaten by a hungry fox, if they need to!

In the wild, most skunks live for 3 years. Skunks that are kept in zoos can live up to 15 years.

Another Smelly Defense

Skunks aren't the only animals that use a bad smell to protect themselves. The fulmar is a seabird that not only smells really bad but spits a stinky oil at its enemies.

When the fulmar spits the disgusting oil, it sticks to its enemies' feathers or fur. It's so sticky that it becomes hard for the animals to move or fly away. Luckily, if the fulmar gets oil on its own feathers, it's able to clean itself.

Glossary

dens (DENZ)
homes aboveground or belowground where skunks rest and hide from enemies

enemies
(EN-uh-meez)
animals that hunt other animals for survival

grasslands
(GRASS-landz)
large, open areas of land where grass grows

kits (KITS)
newborn skunks

Index

Read More

Bekkering, Annalise. *Skunks*. New York: Weigl Publishers (2007).

Mason, Adrienne. *Skunks*. Toronto, Canada: Kids Can Press (2006).

Swanson, Diane. *Welcome to the World of Skunks*. Vancouver, Canada: Whitecap Books (1999).

Learn More Online

To learn more about skunks, visit
www.bearportpublishing.com/GrossOutDefenses

About the Author

Catherine Nichols has written many books for children, including several on animals. She lives in upstate New York with her dog and two cats.